The Visitations

A dialogue about change, focus, shame,
getting older, heaven, dignity,
self-respect and other weighty matters.

remembered by
Bob Beverley

I was very hesitant to let this book see the light of day,
partly because it is so much about my own struggles, even
more because it is so hard to do justice to the things talked
about in these pages.
I will rely on mercy and grace, and trust that something
herein helps you more than I can imagine.
And I will rely on you—read this book with yourself in mind,
see what applies to you,
even better, make it apply to you.

Bob Beverley

This is a true story, in a story kind of way.

A woman came to visit me in my psychotherapy office this week and she refused to tell me her name. She was very attentive. She listened so well, in fact, that it was scary. She looked intently at me, but also seemed amused. I know you are going to think that I have finally slipped over the edge, but I am quite sure the woman was Jo-Ann Townsend, one of my favorite teachers from therapy school. The thing is Joanne passed away about ten years ago, during an operation. I didn't even know that she was sick. No one got to say goodbye to her...and now either she or some imposter or some figment of my imagination was saying "Hello again, Bob."

Needless to say, I could barely think straight while having to act as if this was a routine initial counseling appointment. Here is what I remember of our dialogue.....

Bob Beverley

The First Visitation

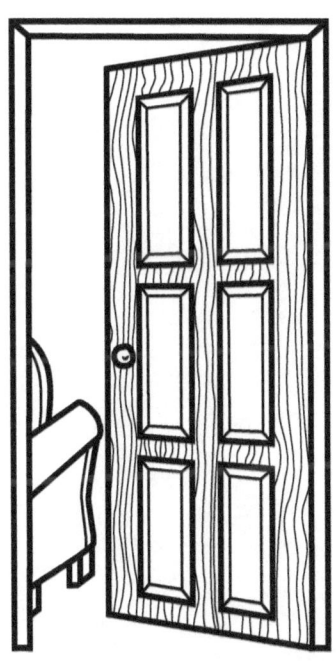

The first visitation from Jo-Ann

Bob: I am very happy to see you, and more than a bit...shocked. Dear friend, why are you here?

Jo-Ann: We can tell you need a break.
You need some insight.

Bob: Who is we?

Jo-Ann: All who care for you. You are getting older. You need to own that fact more, accept it, and yet gently fight it, while letting Father Time teach you more urgency, limits, wisdom and deeper love.

Bob: Deeper love?

Jo-Ann: You know that we do all kinds of ultimately hurtful things in an attempt to find soothing and calm and bliss. We swallow pills, drink to oblivion, and yearn for a thousand people to touch us in tangible ways—and deeper love is the awareness that we are radically and viscerally necessary in the salvation of other people.

Bob: Most of us don't feel very necessary.

Jo-Ann: Yes, that's how we feel, but the truth is each of us is so crucial, so needed, and so vital.

The longer you live the more you realize that the ones who have saved you are the ones who have presented themselves, as in gifting you with their presence in your life. I remember the time my husband drove through a hundred-mile snowstorm because he heard how lonely I was. I remember how my mother would hold me all night when I had migraines. So much human interaction is the opposite of these things —it is talk, gesture, show, emptiness.

Bob: Why are you telling me this?

Jo-Ann: Because every therapist, like every person, can hide behind theories and distance from human pain through familiarity, professional coolness, and safe invulnerable detachment covered over by talk and sentiment and nice wishes.

Bob: As a therapist, isn't some detachment necessary?

Jo-Ann: That's a great theory, isn't it? Too bad it doesn't work. In your work, and in life, it is all - as Freud said - "a cure through love."

Bob: What have you seen of this that you can tell me about, from what you call the other side?

Jo-Ann: The other side is here in every real act of love and in the yearning for a better day, a better moment, a euphoric experience. The search for transcendence is in our tears, our music, our art, and any refusal to give up and give in totally to the darkness.

Bob: So it would seem that there are a lot more people on the side of the angels than is apparent from the dreadful daily news, yes?

Jo-Ann: Yes, but the angels don't like it when people spend a lot of time in guesswork as to who is on their side or not. The real question for every human being is an accountability for everything *they* have seen or known. You've held a baby, you've seen a whale jump out of the water, and you've screamed at a concert, someone has shed blood for you. This all has touched you. What have you done with it? Have you felt the magic and has that magic made a difference?

Bob: I don't feel the magic as much as I used to.

Jo-Ann: You are tired. I admire all that you do, despite your fatigue and anxiety. But you will only find the magic you need for the older years if you rest and focus and become as sharp and precise as the knife that cuts people who want to cut away their pain. And if you soak up all the love that comes your way, because love is the true magic.

Bob: Do you love me?

Jo-Ann: I would not have been sent to you if I did not love you. So, yes, I love you. But don't go off in your head about this or start thinking about anything else.

Bob: Are you real?

Jo-Ann: I am more real than anyone just going through the motions. And know this: right now I am loving you as if you are the only thing that matters and the only thing that exists. This is how the other side loves.

Bob: Tell me more from the other side, more magic.

Jo-Ann: Believe those who differ with your familiar craziness, as if those differing ones are angels from heaven— because they are! Receive every good thing with surprise and gratitude and delight. Living the magic requires practice and intention. The essence is: stop going through the motions. Wake up. Put your heart into things and pay attention and be sharp enough to hear the truth about your craziness and shrewd enough to go down a fresh, new path.

Bob: What can I do for you?

Jo-Ann: You can tell my husband and my daughter that we had this conversation and that we had this time together and you, at the very least, thought of me. And tell them that all things are well and all manner of things shall be well.

The Second Visitation

The second visitation from Jo-Ann

Jo-Ann: You called me back.

Bob: I'm not sure exactly how what you said applies to me.

Jo-Ann: Let's sit in five minutes of silence. Listen to your soul. What does it tell you?

FIVE MINUTES OF SILENCE

Jo-Ann: Time is up. Anything come to you?

Bob: One word keeps coming to me over and over again, but it doesn't sound very pretty.

Jo-Ann: So you get to remember what it's like to sit in the patient's chair and spill the embarrassing beans.
What's the word?

Bob: Ruthless.

Jo-Ann: Oh, that's one of the favorite words on the other side.

Bob: I'm not sure that's comforting.

Jo-Ann: It's scary, but comforting to know that heaven is ruthless towards evil and darkness.

On earth you can see the enormous junk in conversation and culture, the complete missing of the point in a lot of politics, the useless fights over trivia in every sphere of life, and you want to and still can live better—to see what doesn't matter anymore, and to alleviate suffering in your own life and others. Seneca said "Live immediately." Heaven said to you "Be ruthless now."

Bob: Yes, how do you think I should be more ruthless?

Jo-Ann: You MUST assess your life this weekend and DECIDE what ACTIONS you are going to take to make your life even better than it is. The glow from my visit will quickly fade and your needed revolution will disappear in the onslaught of daily life that will carry you away to familiar and comfortable directions. This is your chance, your rehab, and your revelation moment. This is a different day and you need to give way more time to yourself so you can focus on your special gifts, focus on those you love the most, read with purpose, and become, most of all, a person of action.

Bob: Action as in what?

Jo-Ann: You are smart enough to figure that out, but only if you give yourself the time to take care, to slow down, to make space, to ponder and reflect and then to ponder some more-- and then you will see the new things that need to be done. Smart action is preceded by thinking—and by dwelling on your priorities. However, it's not as easy as I make it sound. No therapist alive can accurately assess how slippery and defensive and cunning and duplicitous every human being is.

It is only when you get to the other side and live in utter clarity and openness and joyful soberness that you can begin to surmise the extent and amount of human deviousness. Of course it is part of what makes life very interesting, but it is also impossible to sort out the good and the bad down here with anything approaching truth or justice. Human beings judge so quickly and mostly have no idea of the complexities involved—in the life of a person, the history of a country, or the dirt and glory going on merely inside a town hall. It's funny and sad, all at the same time.

Bob: I'm beginning to worry about Judgment Day.
Is there such a thing?

Jo-Ann: Yes, but it is private screening only, so relax. The wonderful thing is that no one can slip away from THE SERIOUS ONE (that is my private name for Yahweh). And that is why there is nothing but light and fun on the other side, and good work. The B.S. is over. Evil is finished.

Bob: Heaven seems too good to be true.

Jo-Ann: It is better than you can imagine, but isn't this very life too good to be true, at least some of the time?

Bob: Yes, but not for some.

Jo-Ann: Which is why I adore those who long for there to be a heaven, even if they have their doubts. It is a cry for justice, a hopeful wish for those who never stood a chance.

The Third Visitation

A third visitation from Jo-Ann

Bob: You're back, but I did not summon you.

Jo-Ann: Not everything depends on your beck and call. You have been saved many a time by an unanticipated letter in the mail, a surprising visitor to your office, or a grand gesture from a friend. Grace is often unexpected and has its own assertiveness.

Bob: Why are you here?

Jo-Ann: You're the therapist. You tell me.

Bob: I still need lots of help.

Jo-Ann: Always will. Just like everyone else. Nothing to be ashamed of. Normal humanity.

Bob: Why do I feel slightly ashamed about needing lots of help?

Jo-Ann: It's partly because you're the expert who is supposed to have his act together, and not have any serious flaws, let alone mention them in public.

Bob: Yes, but I've always told those I help that I am a failed obsessive, slow to do scary things, and I am screwed up.

Jo-Ann: All those are generalities, relatively easy to say. Kudos to you for not being arrogant, but you are far from a walking afternoon talk show, airing really dirty laundry. You are rightly quite shrewd in what you reveal and what you don't reveal. You always have the client's interest in mind and that is what matters.

Bob: So how can I help them with shame? Do I hang out my specific shame on the clothesline?

Jo-Ann: No, there are enough people doing that. It only seems to bring laughter or mockery. Let me help them and you.

Bob: You're my guest. Go ahead.

Jo-Ann: In my office on the Upper West Side, it often struck me that shame is the first and deepest wound we receive and the last wound we truly face. We are ashamed to face our shame. Because it is so wordless—as you wrote a while ago, it's like "bacon grease drippings of shame." We hide our faces, lower our eyes, keep our problems to ourselves, and in that isolation we become totally convinced that we are as bad as we feel. And then we become bitter and resentful that no one rescues us, when it seems so obvious that we are hanging from a ledge.

Bob: No wonder I loved you as a supervisor. And I loved your office—so minimal, so neat, with the lovely garden outside.

Jo-Ann: Those were the days. The magic of simply waking up, kissing my husband, giving my daughter a hug, walking to work and stepping into my office ready to hear those stories of humanity, often more gripping than fiction. And, at the end of the day, going home for a meal, some music, a good movie, deep talk, and rest and sleep. It is the best. To do any of that almost every day, in safety and freedom, is more of a privilege than much of the world ever gets to know.

Bob: What does this have to do with shame?

Jo-Ann: Everything, everything, everything. I'm talking about the glory of life, the beauty of an ordinary day, a therapist's unquestioned acceptance of the worth inherent in every journey, the love of family and friends, the vast importance of work, the exquisite gifts of music and film and flowers—this is the drenching that wipes away shame, maybe not quickly or totally, but with some degree of force and power.

Bob: What you are saying is the reminder we all need every day.

Jo-Ann: Yes. This is why isolation is often so deadly. In isolation we are taken captive by shame and it drowns out self-glory. Our job is to point out the glory, to name it, and that includes the glory of you, me and all who hear these words.

The Fourth Visitation

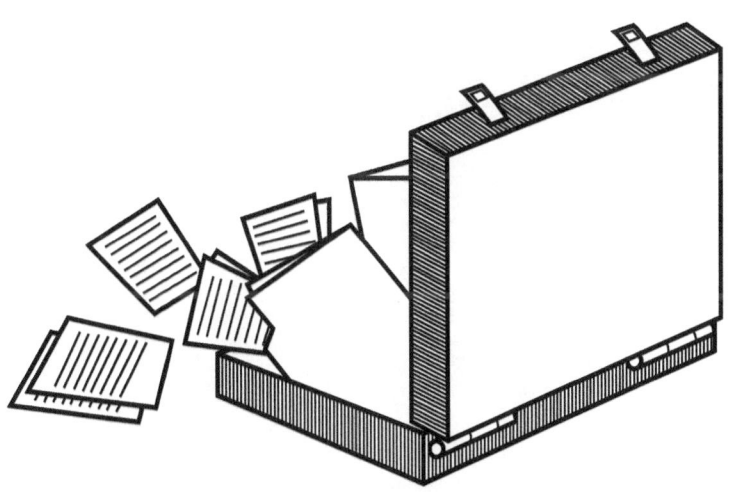

A fourth visitation from Jo-Ann

Jo-Ann: This will be my last visit, and so I want to say many things to you.

Bob: Why is this your last visit?

Jo-Ann: The timing of things is not up to me. And I don't want you or your readers to get used to these visits. Aficionados of the other side dislike familiarity.

Bob: What do you have to say?

Jo-Ann: Do you remember the time your briefcase spilled in my office and I was horrified at all you carried around?

Bob: Your point is that I still carry too much stuff in my briefcase, files, bookshelves, and mind. My ambitions and goals need to be reined in, focused, and gone over ruthlessly, as was told me by heaven in the first visit with you.

Jo-Ann: Exactly. No need to be defensive. As a flaw, I'd settle for it any day. It beats boredom, apathy, any kind of stupor and violence... all to hell. The other side appreciates passion of almost any sort. Indifference is hated more than familiarity, though it is often its result. Passion has to be precise, just like life. Focus is crucial. Focus rests the brain and leads to energy.

Bob: I don't know how to focus more precisely. I like too many things and my work involves lots of diverse and complex pathologies. Besides, there are so many great books and movies and TV shows and blogs. I feel so far behind, almost desperate about it.

Jo-Ann: You are already desperate. Your night stand is starting to look like it did when you wrote about it a while back—as if you are a depository for the Library of Congress.

Bob: What is wrong with me?

Jo-Ann: Every human being is prone to what Freud called "repetitious compulsion." Every human being is greedy, addicted to something, blind to obvious flaws, doing things that amount to a hill of beans, and avoiding and postponing the things that really matter. Every human being gets so used to their folly and pain that the lunacy can go on for decades. You are no different. In fact, you are more messed up than we were hoping.

Bob: Oh dear.

Jo-Ann: Consequently, heaven has decided to be far clearer and more specific with you. I will get to certain matters in a moment, but at this point you need to know I am only going to say things once.

Bob: Why is that?

Jo-Ann: If you know I am only going to say something once, it invites you to be radically alert and sharper. It's a sly way of demanding more of ourselves in speaking and listening and it implicitly invites action.

Bob: I understand. What do I need to hear?

Stop using your cell phone in the car other than to talk and listen. Pull over to dial a number or touch your phone in any way. You have already been given enough warnings about this one to wake a dead horse.

Track your money at least once a week. In detail. Money powers almost everything.

It is amazing that you are a kind and grateful guy given your bone disease: you have broken over twenty bones, ruptured five major tendons or muscles, and had two open heart surgeries, just to name a few details. But you are too used to bodily tightness and pain. Do a lot more to make up for your injuries. Stretch every day. Go for a walk every day. Exercise at least three times a week. Now. Forever.

Heaven wants you to weigh 180 lbs.
by May 17, 2016. (No exact weight given
here as to how much you have to lose.
Heaven is truthful, but not cruel. Grace is
articulate, but discreet.)

You have delicious fantasies of how you want your life to be. Emotional elegance and all that. You write about it so eloquently. We know you write to yourself. Like us all, you have life disorder. Fix it, don't just talk about it or write about it. You will be angry at yourself if you don't get more serious about this. Your life is nothing to be ashamed of—but you want it to be more exquisite. Go for it. Be impatient with those who slow you down.

Your life has been saved by your willingness to seek out feedback, criticism, and affirmation. Despite your tender heart, you have picked the toughest professors and therapists and have always asked your bright friends for candid illumination. Bravo for you. However, every now and then you go "radio silent" especially if you are struggling, and this is a mistake you do not tolerate in your clients. You tell them not to hesitate to call you if they are lonely or have screwed up in some big or small way. You are of the same cloth. You have cobwebs of fogginess that blind you and bacon grease shame that stops you from telling the truth to your friends. Be vulnerable and keep communication open. Your beauty is far greater than your shame.

I saw it when you met me in my office on the Upper West Side 25 years ago. It is even clearer now.

You have seen too much craziness. You are too used to it. Take a step back. See the needless pain. Find ways to be sharper, to be more alarming, to shout, or to quietly get the point across that people need to hear. Don't "just sit there" very long. Once you know the story and once they know you care, be bolder. Evil acts quickly and decisively. You should pick up speed. Speak the truth with love and ruthlessness. Be quicker than evil and as decisive. Lives are at stake.

The above can only be done with an abundance of energy.

Listen to more music. You love it. It takes time (but not that much) to organize your music life. You keep forgetting all that music has meant to you and still means. Remember lying on your back in the living room when you were a teenager listening to The 1812 Overture or Beethoven's 9th? Glory awaits.

I will whisper the most important one to you, so no one else can hear.

Bob: I'm surprised that you did not say anything about sex.

Jo-Ann: I'm not surprised that you noticed. Maybe if I visit again we will talk more about that complexity.

Bob: Is there sex on the other side?

Jo-Ann: There is something better.

Bob: Can you give us a hint?

Jo-Ann: No, like all of heaven, it is beyond any human's grasp. Save your energy for what you need to grasp on this side.

Bob: Any final words for now?

Jo-Ann: In a few days it will be hard to believe that I was here and you can so easily forget what I have said. Cling to what touched you and do what matters so very much more than you know.

Bob: Thank you from the bottom of my heart for visiting me, Jo-Ann.

The Fifth Visitation

Bob: It's been six months. I thought there were going to be no more visits. I'm astonished.

Jo-Ann: No, Bob, whatever you are, you're not astonished. You're already off in your head, seriously wondering what I am doing here, and you are used to me visiting you. And we've figured out that you are also used to almost everything I've told you, because you've been telling yourself some of the same things for years. But do not feel bad about this. It is a simple fact that deep truths get told over and over again and that they lose their impact.

Bob: So where does that leave us?

Jo-Ann: The question is: Where does it leave you?
I wonder what you are feeling about yourself.

Bob: I am a bit disappointed. Your visit didn't make as much difference as I hoped. I know I haven't done as well with your list as I could have.

Jo-Ann: It's not *my* list. It's a list of things that you need to wrestle with, as your soul and heaven told you. I'm here to help, not enforce. Reality is the great enforcer—as are each of us, in terms of our response to reality, or the endless ways we seek to avoid, escape, deny or twist reality.

Bob: Please help me more.

Jo-Ann: How can I help you? What do you need to hear?

Bob: I would think someone from heaven would know.

Jo-Ann: When Jesus was on earth, he always asked people what they wanted and what they were after. I can't do better than him. So...how can I help you?

Bob: I think I'm stuck. Help me get unstuck.

Jo-Ann: You could be stuck, but that word is often a euphemism for a whole mix of things. People who feel stuck are often tired or anxious or depressed or simply on a plateau, none of which is quite the same as, say, a car stuck in the mud, spinning wheels, going nowhere, just getting in a deeper hole. I would not say that describes you at all. Perhaps you think that you are not moving as fast as you should be, to where you want to be with your goals, in your heart, in your life?

Bob: Yes, that's more like it.....so, how can I get to be where I want to be faster?

Jo-Ann: The ironic thing is that you have to slow way down in order to get what you want...faster. You have to stop and listen to your heart to know what you really, really want. You have to be still long enough to examine your life, to get your bearings, to look at the roads you are taking and not taking, to feel where you are being pulled, to feel your soul's longing, to know what you are sick of, to know deep in your heart what really matters to you. It not only takes time to do all this, to take care, as we say—it also takes courage because it can be painful to see how far off the path you are, or it takes courage to be an individual and live the unique life you desire.

Bob: I think I feel vague guilt when I focus so much time on myself.

Jo-Ann: Heaven knows it should be the other way round—seriously, you don't take enough time to look after your own life, to do for your life what only you can do. Yes, as you taught us, people look after their lives by taking care of others, and that is the easiest and best way to find meaning. However, you have to take care of yourself along the lines heaven has already told you. It's no different than a surgeon operating on your body. You receive all his or her attention for whatever time it takes. It's your turn on the table. It's the same with your soul and the details of your life. You have to be your own surgeon and attend to the demands and details of your daily existence...and the dreams of your soul. This is a must, the way life is. You matter too.

Bob: None of this sounds so miraculous that anyone would believe me if I told them that all your words came from someone who has seen the other side.

Jo-Ann: The words are meant for you, not to prove anything to anyone else. If the words are of divine origin, they will fit, they will be true, and they will save you, even though the words might not light up a Broadway stage. The process of salvation is often not dramatic. Heaven touches the earth in mostly ordinary ways, and it is fatally easy to miss the ordinary, to not take the next step that looks so unimportant.

For example, heaven's advice about cell phones would not make the front page of any newspaper. You would be deemed a fool if you told other people that God visited you so that you would never text and drive. However, it could save your life.

Bob: I feel less guilty about the time spent on me, but what can you tell me that will help others?

Jo-Ann: Nice try. I'm not playing that game. I was sent here for the sole purpose of talking to you. If you want to help people, that's your prerogative—but my mission is to help you.

Bob: It will help me to help others.

Jo-Ann: Well, then, you go ahead and help them? What do you need to say to any who might read our dialogue?

Bob: Since you don't seem that interested, I will be brief.

Jo-Ann: It's not that I'm not interested. I was sent by The Serious One to get through to you. There is something slightly "off" in how you live. Again, you're not a walking disaster or living in utter delusion. But you refuse to take enough time to fix the things that you say you want to fix. The simple truth may be that you do not have enough time, but the days are passing and (up to this point) you do not seem very urgent about the urgent matters that have been brought to your attention. As long as you helping others is not a diversion or distraction from what you need to do, I'm fine with your intent. Please...

Bob: Here is what I would tell people if I was an angel from heaven:

Make a list of all the people who matter to you and do something for one of them every day on a rotation basis—a quick phone call, an email, a letter, a thank you, a big and generous gift of creative beauty. They all need a surprise gesture of love just as much as you do. These acts of goodness will lift your heart and mood as well.

Be aware that every day you are building a foundation that will either make your life easier or harder, possibly for decades to come.

If you are thinking of doing something that might be foolish, phone me and talk about the pros and cons. I've heard it all and can help you figure things out. 845-417-5486

Action is the key to sanity. Keep doing what you know you need to do, exercise a lot, and stay away from the depressing chair or bed where the devil can easily hold you down you in chains.

Constant fighting with your partner is far worse than you can imagine. Everything is advertising, even in relationships.

The mission and purpose you have been looking for is right in front of you. Who needs your help today?

Be kinder to your employees. If you are wealthy, it is a crime not to pay back those who have made you wealthy. All work is sacred. Thinking only of yourself will make you poor and afraid.

If you are an employee, understand that being an owner is not as easy as it looks. Give your best, and if your boss is not worthy of you, look elsewhere.

The misuse of alcohol and drugs are the devil's most cunning weapons. If you know this to be true, if you understand the seductive illusion of such misuse and, even more, understand the beauty of sober living, please tell us or write a book about it. Until then, read "In Love With Daylight: A Memoir of Recovery" by Wilfrid Sheed.

If you are a world leader, imagine anew that every person you deal with is someone's child, as precious to them as your life is to you.

Jo-Ann: Those are all crucial insights, and if people followed them, there would be far less pain. I would like you to tell me something else, which is perhaps imbedded in what you said just now. What do you really believe? What is sacred for you? Where has the Divine touched you?

Bob: Do you know my usual caveats in this regard?

Jo-Ann: I think so. You were a philosophy major and that sent permanent waves of doubt down your spine. Your holy job dips you deep in the world's evil every week and so you do not glibly talk about God as if the Lord is your or anyone's personal valet! Sometimes God seems a very absent help in trouble. Catastrophe is all over the place. Is that what you mean?

Bob: Yes.

Jo-Ann: Good for you. The other day I heard a Christian talk about the evil of Muslim terrorists and in the next breath she casually mentioned about how her brother-in-law died a terrible death from cancer, but he (in her distinct and certain opinion) was not a Christian and was in hell, because you don't get to heaven by being a Boy Scout. It's a good thing it was a social occasion. I felt like slapping her across the face. It's talky Christian terrorism. Ugh.

Bob: I've seen that a thousand times. No wonder Richard Dawkins and crew are such fundamentalists about atheism. Believers give them lots of ammo.

Jo-Ann: But enough with our negativity. What light have you seen? Caveats accepted. What is holy for you?

Bob: The word salvation has to do with a root word that means soothing. Words like sacred and holy refer to times or places or people or moments or things that are enchanting and luminous and hallowed and cherished and revered. This time with you has been like that for me, of course. Despite my disappointment in myself, and despite my doubt that you are really here, I am so, so touched that you came to me in this way. By the way, I wanted to tell you that I talked to your husband and he was more than delighted to hear that we had these conversations.

Jo-Ann: You can probably see the tears in my eyes.
Thank you.

Bob: You are most welcome....I especially believe every baby is holy, that children are magic, and after that, all bets are off. I know you can see good and evil in all people—we all need grace and mercy, we all deserve and need judgement. (In healthy theology, judgement is a confirmation of honor—we are worthy of being judged, we are not leaves under the feet of the Divine, mere sports for the gods.) I believe every good thing is sacred, except we can barely see it most of the time. We forget so much, forget what we have seen. Religion, at its best, is a deliberate attempt to remember what we have seen. I think words are sacred tools and I know, beyond the shadow of a doubt, that quotations and thoughts and books have been sacraments for me.

When I was a depressed teenager, I discovered sex in all its (at that time) handy glory, and though I do not have the skill to write about it, nor do my kids want to read this, sexual pleasure and orgasms are so soothing, so comforting, so full of love (it always is, at least in our head), that it begs to be mentioned. I have heard a few ministers speak who were justly famous (Billy Graham, the famous evangelist; D. Martyn Lloyd-Jones, British preacher, former surgeon to the Queen of England; Bob Cook of King's College, Nyack, N.Y.) and holiness seemed as thick as smoke in the rooms where I heard them. I felt that these people had spent a long time in the presence of something inexplicable. Something that evoked awe. And then there's all the stories we hear, that seem to be from reliable sources, that can't be explained by anything other than "there's a divinity that shapes our ends, rough-hew them how we will," as Shakespeare wrote.

Finally, in this all too brief list, I simply cannot believe that this whole gorgeous, complex world exists by mindless accident. Maybe this shows the depth of my ignorance, but the world, despite all its evil and flaws, looks created to me, full of wonder and beauty that is simply staggering.

Jo-Ann: How does your psychotherapy work shape your view of divinity?

Bob: It is plain as day that every person's life is very much a battle between good and evil, between love and indifference, between those who are Christ for us and those who can't be bothered. I hear sacred stories every week in my holy room—stories of forgiveness, stories of people asserting their worth, stories of people turning their lives around, one rough step at a time. I see tears of joy and sorrow, regret as deep as the ocean, loneliness that beckons my love, and the soul's longing to be heard and noticed and attended to. It is all sacred beyond measure. As St. Paul wrote, "Who is sufficient for these things?" As C.S. Lewis said, we all have "a weight of glory" around us.

Jo-Ann: What kind of stories were you referring to that reminded you of a divinity that shapes our ends?

Bob: A fellow therapist told me this story. One of his female clients wakes in the early morning hours and a voice tells her that her brother has a ruptured appendix and will die if he doesn't have emergency surgery. This is very odd, nothing like this had ever happened to her. Despite how weird it seemed, she called her brother even though he was on the west coast and it would be the middle of the night. He answered the phone immediately, heard what she had to say and replied "I'm in the emergency room with terrible abdominal pain." She told him "Tell the doctors you have a ruptured appendix and you need an operation." They did an emergency CAT scan and discovered the voice was right. This saved her brother's life.

Jo-Ann: How lovely.

Bob: Do you disagree with anything I've said?

Jo-Ann: No, I would emphasize it even more in your life and work, because what touches us deeply is the easiest path to transformation. What touches us is a gift...and those touches we can move towards, and other times they come out of the blue, often from the most unexpected places or people.

Bob: Like you visiting me. Thank you once again.

Afterword....to my readers

These visitations with Jo-Ann Townsend gave me a chance to reflect on my own life as well as to honor her memory. I hope that "The Visitations" helps you to live more sharply, with more magic, and with an eye out for what touches you, for what has been or will be sacred in your life.

If you read this book and you are my client, you must promise to discuss any significant issue that might arise in you, or between us, because I revealed a bit more of myself than usual in these pages. And thanks for being my client!

If you are interested in further reading, I recommend Frederick Buechner "The Sacred Journey" and "Eyes of the Heart: A Memoir of the Lost and Found"; Francis Spufford "Unapolegetic: Why, Despite Everything, Christianity can still make Surprising Emotional Sense."

Thanks to my smart, compassionate friends who gave me valuable feedback about this project. I am grateful to Kyle Perry from Perry Creative Design Company for the layout and artwork; and likewise grateful to Ion Zupcu of Ion Zupcu Photography for the pleasure of watching a master at his craft.